Dominie Marine Life

Monsters of the Deep

Contents

Text by Stanley L. Swartz
Photography by Robert Yin

DOMINIE PRESS
Pearson Learning Group

Are They Monsters?

There are stories about monsters that live deep in the ocean. One story tells about a giant creature that ate a whole ship. **Science** can help us learn about these animals. Are they really monsters?

◀ Crocodile fish

Octopuses

An octopus has eight long arms. There are some stories about octopuses that have attacked **divers**. Actually, these animals are shy and playful.

 Octopus

When an octopus is afraid or angry, it can change color. This can make it look very **frightening**. White means fear. Red is for anger.

◀ Octopus

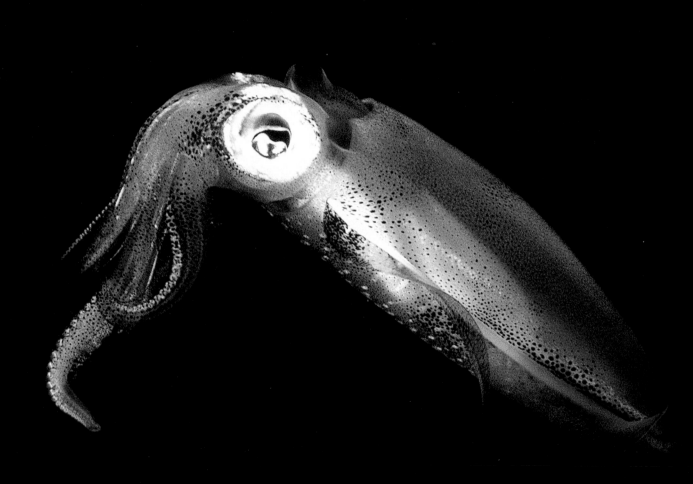

Squid

The squid is related to the octopus. Some squid are **luminous**. They seem to glow. Flying squid can jump twenty feet out of the water. Some flying squid have jumped onto boats.

 Squid

Barracuda

The barracuda is a fierce **predator**. It has long, pointed teeth. The barracuda sits very still and waits for its prey. When it sees a fish it wants to eat, it quickly attacks.

◀ Barracuda

Manta Rays

Manta Rays are gentle giants that can weigh more than 3,000 pounds. They are harmless unless they are **provoked**. One fisherman caught a Manta Ray by accident. His boat almost sank when the ray took a deep dive.

◀ Manta Ray

Sharks

The word *shark* brings fear to many people. But most sharks will not hurt people. The Whitetip Shark feeds mostly on the bottom of the ocean or around **coral reefs**. The shark's greatest enemy is another shark.

◀ **Whitetip Shark**

Sea Snakes

Sea snakes breathe air. They are found in **shallow** water and are poisonous. A sea snake can swallow a fish that is twice as big as the sea snake's neck.

◀ Sea Snake

Moray Eels

The Moray Eel looks like a snake. It wiggles through the water. It hunts close to the bottom and uses smell and touch to find food. The Moray Eel is **nocturnal**. It looks for food at night.

◀ Moray Eel

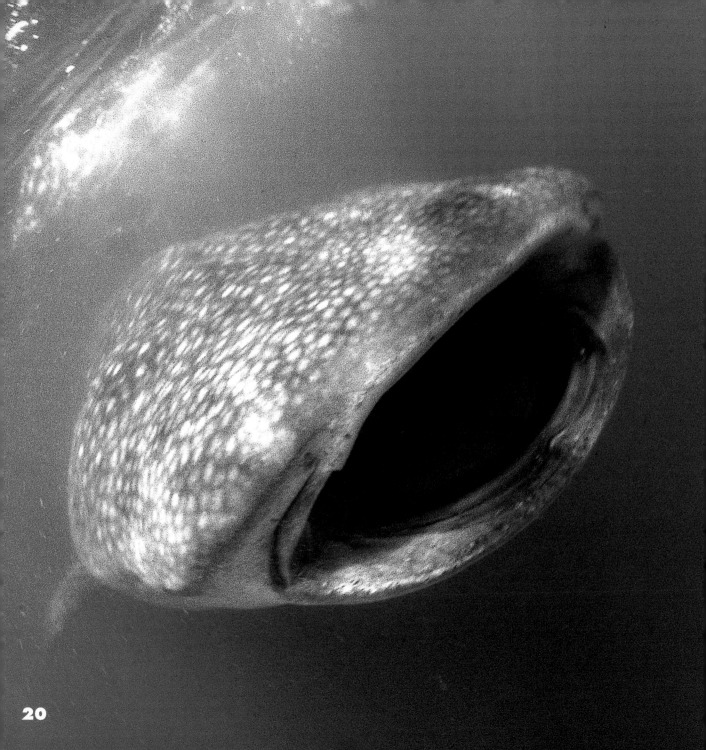

Whale Sharks

The Whale Shark is the largest fish in the world. It can grow to be more than forty feet long and weigh more than fifteen **tons**. That is as much as three elephants. The mouth of a Whale Shark can be up to four feet wide.

◄ **Whale Shark**

Gentle Creatures

We have read that monsters of the deep are not monsters at all. Most are **gentle** creatures that do not harm humans. Science helps us learn the facts about these interesting creatures.

◀ **Whale Shark**

Glossary

coral reefs: Hard shelves of coral

divers: People who work underwater; Robert Yin is a diver who took the photographs for this book.

frightening: Something that is scary

gentle: Mild and soft

luminous: Filled with light; bright and glowing

nocturnal: Having to do with night

predator: An animal that hunts and kills other animals

provoked: Angry or upset

science: The study of the natural world

shallow: Not deep

ton: One ton is 2,000 pounds

Index